LINDOS

NANNO MARINATOS
Dr. OF ARCHAEOLOGY

LINDOS

ARCHAEOLOGY - HISTORY - RELIGION

TOURIST GUIDE

AND EXTRA

RECONSTRUCTION OF THE ACROPOLIS

ATHENS 1985

Γενικός ἀντιπρόσωπος Ρόδου: Σίμος Κοέν
Διεύθυνση: Πλ. Ἱπποκράτους 14
Τηλέφωνο: 22.005, 23.940

LINDOS

HISTORICAL BACKGROUND

Many of the ancient myths about Rhodes connect the island with gods or heroes who passed through. The gods Apollo and Artemis visited Rhodes, the hero Danaos fleeing from Egypt, Herakles and his son Tlepólemos, and Kadmos the Phoenician stopped in Rhodes on their way to other places. The legends and myths point to the important geographical position of the island, which undoubtedly was the most crucial factor in its development.

Prehistoric Times

Since we have no written historical records for the Bronze Age (3000-1100 BC), we have to rely on the archaeological evidence.

Rhodes seems to have been a colony of the Minoans ever since the protopalatial period in Crete (c. 1800 BC). The Minoans developed a thalassocracy, a domination of the seas, which reached its peak in the early 15th cent. BC. They founded colonies and brought most of the islands of the Aegean under their sphere of influence. In Rhodes, they colonized the area of Trianda and perhaps had a sanctuary on the Acropolis of Ialysos. When the Minoan power declined, another power emerged, the Mycenaeans, who were the inhabitants of the mainland and who spoke an early from of Greek. They more or less inherited the Minoan empire and settled in places which the Minoans had previously occupied. In Rhodes, they settled on the northern part of the island. Extensive cemeteries in the areas of Ialysos and Kameiros testify to their presence. According to certain scholars, the Mycenaeans (or Achaeans) of Rhodes are referred to in the Hittite texts, which testifies to the importance of the Mycenaean power on the island. Of course, the geographical position of the island, so close to the coast of Asia Minor, made it an important base for Mycenaean contacts abroad, and we know that the Mycenaeans had an extensive trade network in the East.

Around 1200 BC, the major powers in the East, including Egypt, suffered a great blow by hordes of wandering peoples known collectively as the Sea Peoples. Their mass migration, causing destruction and looting, disrupted the smooth trade operations of the Mycenaeans and their power began to decline. After a period of chaos, a new wave of Greeks, known as the Dorians, migrated from the NW and settled on the mainland and many of the islands. Around the 10th century Rhodes received such a wave of colonizers as well as Crete. The Dorians brought with them new institutions and new customs, but it is important to remember that although they spoke a different dialect, they basically spoke the same language as the Mycenaeans, namely Greek. This means that a certain assimilation of the old and the new took place, notably in the field of religion. More will be said about that in the section on cults.

Greek Historical Times

The Dorians settled on three major sites, Ialysos, Kameiros and Lindos, which soon attained a high level of cultural prosperity. Together with a Dorian state in Kos and two on the coast of Asia Minor (Knidos and Halikarnassos) they formed the Dorian **hexapolis** (six cities). These cities played an important role in the development of Classical Greek art and literature. This is because Greek civilization constantly drew and got inspired from the Eastern cultures, with which the coastal cities of Asia Minor and the islands came increasingly in contact. Halikarnassos was the birthplace of Herodotus, the father of history.

Rhodes flourished in the 8th cent. BC, a period which has recently been designated as the «Greek Renaissance». During this century and the following ones, the 7th 6th cent. the Greeks came into closer contact with the Eastern world and, as we have noted above, this was crucial for the development of Greek civilization. Rhodes traded with Attica, the East and Crete and thus became the centre of an important network. The Phoenician alphabet was taken over by the Greeks probably on the island of Cyprus and was soon spread over the rest of Greece. Rhodes was one of the first islands to adopt the script, as we can see from the very early inscriptions found there. Rhodes was active in another movement: colonization. Either because of overpopulation, or because the emerging aristocracy fought internally (compare with wars of feudal aristocracy, like the War of the Roses in the medieval period), many Greek cities founded colonies abroad. These colonies were independent from the mother-city but they offered obvious commercial advantages. Rhodes chose to colonize in the west in collaboration with Crete, and founded Gela in Sicily. The choice of Sicily in the West was obviously dictated by the need to controll a Western commercial route. Another Rhodian colony was Phaselis, on the coast of Pamphylia (in Asia Minor).

Art in the 8th-6th cent.

In the field of art, Rhodes excelled. Towards the end of the 8th cent., she produced pottery, where birds were the predominant motif. Influences from Attica and Corinth are discernible, whereas contacts with Crete and Cyprus can be testified by imported pots found in the graves of the period. The shapes of the pottery indicate that they were to a great extent drinking vessels (jars for the storage of wine and cups for drinking).

Perhaps they should be interpreted in connection with certain feasts, the **symposia**, which were the vehicles for the expression of wealth and gregariousnes of the aristocracy. Aristocrats competed with each-other in pride and status and the one who could furnish the most lavish feast gained in prestige in the eyes of the others. The lively tradition in pottery continues in the 6th cent., when another style developed, peculiar to Greece, known as the **Fikellura** style. The characteristic shape is the squat amphora (a two-handled jar) with motifs of animals and birds predominating. Especially prominent are «chasing motifs», that is wild animals like panthers, lions etc. chasing their victims. This iconography, prevalent throughout the Greek world in the 7th cent., is Oriental in character, one of many Oriental elements in Greek art.

Towards the end of the 6th cent., Rhodes issued her own coinage according to some scholars. The island seems to have reached an especially high level of prosperity under the tyrant Kleoboulos, who was listed among the «seven wise men» in antiquity, which points to the positive name he left for posterity. In reality Kleoboulos, was a tyrant . A few things should be mentioned about tyranny as a phenomenon of the Archaic period (7th and 6th cent. BC). Many Greek cities, with Sparta as the notable exception, underwent tyranny in the 7th or 6th cent. BC. Tyrants were absolute rulers: they rose to power with illegitimate means, often using the newly formed army system (there was no organized military before the Archaic period) to back them up. Why tyranny spread in this very period is an interesting problem. It probably has to do with the rise of the middle classes, the spread of wealth to a broader section of the population and with the resulting tension between the classes. Thus, tyrants should be seen as the champions of the middle and agrarian classes against the aristocracy. There is good evidence that tyrants were popular in their times, because they backed up the middle classes and broke the monopoly of power enjoyed by the aristocracy. In this way they paved the road for democracy. It is no accident that democracy was established in Athens at the end of the 6th cent., right after a period of tyranny by the Peisistratids. Thus we understand Kleoboulos' reputation as one of the seven wise

General view of the acropolis of Lindos
with the village and the harbour. $\longrightarrow$

men. Actually we know very little about him, but a new temple of Athena Lindia is attributed to his reign. This accords very well with what we know about tyrants. They indulged in impressive building programs, a means to impress the people and provide employment. Perhaps it is no coincidence that the tyranny of Kleoboulos coincides with a prosperous economic development, an exciting style in the pottery (Fikellura) and the erection of the temple of Athena Lindia.

In the early 5th cent., Greece was threatened by the expansion of another major power in the East: Persia. One of the first targets of Persian expansionism was east Greece, and Rhodes fell victim to it at an early stage. The Greeks put up a resistance to the Persian invasion, and the two armies fought several battles. The crucial one was the naval engagement by the island of Salamis, where the Athenian navy played a decisive role. The Persians relied very much on the fleet of their subjects and their allies, the Phoenicians. The Rhodians, being under Persian rule, had to fight on the side of the Persians in the battle of Salamis, which took place in 480 BC. The superiority of Greek tactics and the greater agility of the Greek ships resulted in a decisive victory. After another battle, that of Platea in 479 BC., the Persians withdrew their forces and left the Aegean to the Greeks. Now, however, imperialistic and expansionistic tendencies were manifested among the Greek city-states themselves. Athens became the leader of the newly liberated Greeks, among whom were the Rhodians. However, things took a turn for the worse. By the middle of the 5th cent., Athens became a ruthless imperialistic power under the leadership of Pericles. It is an irony of history that at the time of her most liberal democracy, Athens was a tyrant-state towards her allies, which should be better termed subjects. Among the subjects of Athens were the Cyclades and many islands near the coast of Asia Minor, like Rhodes. Athenian imperialism soon led to a clash with her rival, Sparta. The two cities got involved in a protracted war, the Peloponnesian war, 431-404. Towards the end of the war, when Athens was sufficiently weakened, Rhodes revolted from the yoke in 411 BC. and resumed her Dorian connections with Sparta. This is one of the many testimonies to the unpopularity of the Athenian empire.

In 408 the three cities in Rhodes, Lindos, Ialysos and Kameiros combined to found a federal city on the N. tip of the island, calling it Rhodos. This became the most important city, and it is still the capital today, having survived various conquests by Christians and Moslems. Even the streets of modern Rhodos are reminiscent of the ancient city-planning. The choice of the spot for the city of Rhodos was undoubtedly dictated by reasons of geography. It possesses five harbours, which were an important factor in its subsequent commercial development. The new city had its own administration: the assembly of the people (**ekklesia**) and the administrative council (**boule**), but the other cities (Lindos, Kameiros, Ialysos) retained their autonomy as well. An important magistrate in the city-administration of Rhodos was the priest of the Sun (Helios). This divinity remained

10

important throughout antiquity in Rhodes, and one of the myths associated with the island, makes it a possesion of the sun-god Helios.

Before we leave the 5th cent., a few words should be said about art as it is represented on Rhodes.

From the 5th cent., comes the funeral relief monument of Krito and Timaresta, (Fig. 1) on display in the archaeological Museum of Rhodes. It was set above the grave of the dead woman, Timaresta, who is standing to the right. We can identify her as the dead because she is normally bigger than the other woman. It is a typical farewell scene at the moment of death. The two female figures are not individualized portraits of the particular women in question but types as was the convention in the Classical period. The warrior, the youth, the older man, the mother, the unwed virgin who «marries death» are some of the most frequent types represented. The dead is either alone or, more frequently, accompanied by another person: a member of the family, or a servant. In this particular case it is mother and daughter, an indication of the special bond that they had. Neither the dead, nor the living person displays any strong emotion especially not on the face. Body language is suggestive of restrained grief. Pathos and theatrical gestures do not become popular until later, in the Hellenistic period. The dead looks often detached, as though he/she is already in a differend world, while the living looks subdued and sad. Perhaps it is this restraint on the face of death which renders the funerary monuments of the Classical period particularly moving. Because when the modern spectator confronts them, he can look beyond the specific fate of Timaresta to a fate which is common to us all and admire human dignity at its most sublime form.

The 4th cent. was a period of anarchy and relative decadence in the political sphere for the Greek mainland, but not so for Rhodes, whose prosperity increased even more. However, the political instability of the times is reflected in Rhodes' local history also.

What happened is this. The Peloponnesian War ended in defeat for Athens, whereas Sparta emerged as a victorious power. But things did not stop there. Many competitors for succession appeared, among which were Thebes and a revived Athens. The latter began rebuilding her resources. In the meantime Persia was still powerful and wealthy, whereas an independent Persian satrapy Caria on the coast of Asia Minor, was also strong and had desings on Rhodes. In brief, one can describe the political history of the 4th cent. as a long struggle between the city-states of the Greek mainland until they wore themselves out and fell prey to the outsiders. It so happened that the eventual conqueror was the father of Alexander the Great: Philip of Macedon, but it could well have been Persia. What was Rhodes' position in all this? First she joined the Athenian confederacy in 377, but not long afterwards she switched alliances and joined the Theban alliance which emerged victorious over Sparta. It was Thebes who delivered the final blow to Spartan supremacy. It seems that at first Rhodes was playing the political

1. *The funerary stele of Kritos and Timaristas, from the necropolis of Kamiros. Two women, Timaristas the mother and Kritos her daughter, embrace before parting forever (5th century BC).*

game rather well, but after the middle of the 4th cent. she was not so lucky. The powerful ruler of Caria, Mausolos, managed to get control of Rhodes by installing an oligarchical government, which looked after his interests. The same policy was followed by his successor Artemisia. The attachment of Rhodes to the Carian prince can be interpreted differently also: as a result of Rhodes' discontent with Athens and a desire for a final break with the Athenian confederacy. This was getting to be oppressive and tending towards imperialism, as it was before, in the 5th cent. History was repeating itself. The outcome was different this time, however. Perhaps because the city-states had weakened in the 4th cent., Athens never managed to consolidate her power, as she had done in the 5th cent. In 354 she was forced to recognize the independence of Rhodes, Chios and Kos.

To the political crisis that the mainland went though was added an economic and social one. There was shortage of food and increasing unemployment, which forced young Greek men to look for jobs abroad. Many served as mercenaries in the Persian army, for example. This sort of crisis did not affect Rhodes directly, but since her fate to a certain extent depended on the mainland, political and social developments had repercussions on Rhodian history as well. Because of the crisis described above, the independent city-states of the mainland could not resist the expansionism of the Macedonians led by Philip. There were attempts at resistance, of course. The Athenian politician Demosthenes fought vehemently against Philip with his inspiring speeches in the Athenian asembly. He said that the freedom and independence of the Greek cities was threatened with extinction. He was right. After the conquest of Philip, the Greek city-states suffered a decline and ceased to produce original works of art, literature and philosophy. A new era began, for better or worse. Perhaps the course of events could not have been avoided, however, and given the circumstances, it was better to have Philip than a Persian king.

After Philip's death, his son Alexander undertook to subjugate Persia. The Rhodians allied themselves with him, showing remarkable foresight, since some of the other Greek cities continued feeble attempts at revolt from the Macedonian yoke, which made Alexander mistrustful towards them, but the Rhodians gained a lot from the alliance. The foundation of the city of Alexandria in Egypt by Alexander was of great importance for the commercial contacts between Rhodes and Egypt. As Alexander succeeded in conquering the vast Persian territory bit by bit, he opened more and more markets for the flow of Greek goods and vice versa. Rhodes gained in commercial prosperity without having been weakened by the crisis, from which the mainland suffered. It was in the 4th cent. that a new temple of Athena Lindia was built, as well as the Popylaia, the gates to the temple.

After the death of Alexander his empire was split and a new scene for political struggles was set, in which the successors of Alexander fought for supremacy.

13

The most important kingdoms were Syria, including all the eastern parts of Alexander's empire and part of Asia Minor, Egypt and Macedonia, of which Greece was still a part. These kingdoms are called **Hellenistic,** and the term is also applied to the whole period following Alexander's death until the final conquest of the Greek areas by Rome. (c. 330-30 BC.)

During the struggles between the different dynasties, Rhodes had to pay a price also. Demetrios Poliorketes (the besieger), who was a Macedonian king, fought against Ptolemy, king of Egypt. It was a typical dynastic struggle prompted by greed for more power. Demetrios wanted Rhodes to take his side, and when the Rhodians refused, the king besieged the city o Rhodos in 305. But the «Besieger» (who had gained this reputation in former enterprises) did not manage to take the city. In antiquity, it was extremely difficult to take a fortified city, except by treachery; only Alexander managed to take Tyre. The siege of Rhodes was an important event in her history. With characteristic commercial instinct, the Rhodians sold the siege machines left behind by Demetrios and used the money to build an enormous statue of Helios (the sun-god). This statue has not been preserved but was famous in antiquity because of its colossal size. It is called the **Colossus of Rhodes** and it stood over the entrance of the harbour. (Fig. 2)

In the next centuries of the Hellenistic period, Rhodes reached the height of her cultural prosperity. Needless to repeat that her geographical position, which had always given her some advantages, became even more advantageous in a period when commercial exchange proceeded more smoothly, given the essential unity of the Hellenistic world. Before the Hellenistic period, the Persians had excluded Greek traders from inner Asia. The conquest of this territory by Alexander, the many new cities, the accumulation of wealth in the hands of the middle classes, all gave commerce a tremendous impulse. In antiquity, there was no risk of not finding a market for accumulated goods. A merchant could make a fortune, provided he could find the goods.

Another factor was the shift of trade from Greece to Egypt, Rhodes and the coast of Asia. Alexandria became the centre of spice trade, and Rhodes acted as her depot for expot. Thus, Rhodes developed as a transit trade station, although she had also her own goods to export, notably wine. She was exclusive with her inhabitants too. Among the city-states, only Rhodes and Kyzikos kept out non-Greeks, which was unusual in the cosmopolitan atmosphere of the Hellenistic period. Normally, foreign traders, who settled in a city, formed an association and brought their own goods, But Rhodes wanted no foreigners and no competition in her market.

2. The Colossus was the work of the Lindian sculptor Chares.

Although banking in our sense did not exist, letters of credit were known, and measures were taken to facilitate trade through credit. The international coinage introduced by Alexander also did a lot for trade. By the 3rd cent. BC. the world was divided into two main currency spheres. As an area of transit, Rhodes profited enormously by the circumstances of the Hellenistic period.

In 227 BC. Rhodes was struck by a very severe earthquake. Interestingly enough, a kind of social wellfare system operated in antiquity, which took the form of charity. Other cities and monarchs of Hellenistic kingdoms collected money and sent it to help the island rebuild her city. The great Colossus was also destroyed during this earthquake. The Rhodians were able to rebuild their city on a more lavish scale than before but they never reerected their Colossus, perhaps because they needed the money for something else. It is also worth pointing out that Rhodes had a strong commercial fleet in the Hellenistic period, for which the island had excellent harbours. Lindos especially had secret harbours hidden in caves, which made suitable hiding places in case of attack by an enemy force.

The 2nd cent. BC saw the gradual mingling or Rome in the eastern Mediterranean. Being invited to take sides in the struggles between the various Hellenistic monarchs, she ultimately took over. In 166 BC, Rome broke Rhodes' commercial power by making the island of Delos a free port, i.e. abolishing import and export duties. Although Rhodes did not become bankrupt, Delos took over as a centre of transit trade, and a kind of decline set in.

Rome's involvement in the eastern Mediterranean had further implications: the arrival of the Roman trader. At first he was not unpopular. He often married a Greek wife and integrated in the community. But later, Romans acquired enormous advantages over the Greek merchants, being protected by special laws. Another factor made Romans unpopular: they gradually began regarding the Greek cities as gold-mines of art to be plundered and exploited by the conquerors. Thus Rhodes was sacked by Cassius, one of the murderers of Julius Caesar. The looting was probably done in order for him to raise money to support his army against Caesar's avengers, Octavian and Mark Anthony. Still, it shows the lack of scruples that Romans showed towards Greeks from the 2nd cent. BC onwards. Roman politics had not been exploitative before that, and some historians trace the decline and fall of the Roman Republic in this very attitude of exploitation, which the Roman middle classes developed towards the East against the wishes of the conservative aristocracy.

The Hellenistic period was one of great artistic achievement for Rhodes. At Lindos, the great Doric portico was added to give splendour to the sanctuary and serve as an art gallery. But it was mostly in the field of sculpture that Rhodes

3. The Laokoon group in the Vatican Museum, Rome is one of the most famous pieces of ancient art.

made her greatest impact. Here a few pieces only will be described, some of which can be seen in he Archaeological Museum of the town of Rhodes.

The Laokoon group (in the Vatican Museum, Rome) (Fig. 3) is one of the most famous pieces of ancient act. It depicts the deadly struggle between the priest of Apollo, Laokoon, and his sons on the one side and terrible serpents on the other.

According to the myth, Laokoon tried to persuade his compatriots, the Trojans not to accept the Greek gift of a Wooden Horse into Troy because that would bring destruction. The gods got angry that he was spoiling their plans and sent two deadly serpents to kill him and his sons. When the Trojans witnessed his death, they assumed that he was punished for impiety so they ordered the horse into the city. This was their destruction and Laokoon proved correct. This myth, which expresses man's impotence to change his fate, stimulated the imagination of the Hellenistic artist. Man struggles with the daemonic forces that overpower him. One of Laokoon's sons is looking to his father for help, but the father is too involved in his own death-struggle to be able to help his child. The expression of human agony and pain on the faces of the humans have made this group one of the most representative works of its age, an age which, like ours, stressed individual emotion and suffering. It differs very much from the serene and more somber specimens of the Classical period. For the reasons described above, the Laokoon group acted as a source of inspiration for the Renaissance artists as well (Michelangelo worked on it) and formed a link between antiquity and modern times. It is dated to the middle of the 1rst cent. BC.

The Nike (Victory) of Samothrace (in the Louvre, Paris) (Fig. 4) is a votive figure, which the Rhodians dedicated to the sanctuary of the Kabeirioi after their victory against Antiochos in 190 BC. The name of the sculptor was Pythokritos. This sculpture differs from the Laokoon in conception, and the effect is very different. The Laokoon evokes pathos and pity in the spectator, the Nike delight in the graceful form. It thus exhibits another aspect of Hellenistic art: grace and beauty. The Nike was standing on a ship's prow and is about to fly as the wind blows her dress against her body. The effect is striking, because the heavy texture of the marble is worked to such an extent that we get the illusion of transparent material. This effect was already achieved towards the end of the archaic period (6th cent. BC.) by the Greeks and got perfected as time went on. One need only compare the Nike with the static and massive Egyptian sculpture to appreciate the effect. The artist of the Nike has also managed to capture a moment in time. A modern author has described her as «a headless lady hurrying to catch a bus...»

The Crouching Aphrodite (in the Rhodes Museum) (Fig. 5) is a variant of a well-known type of the goddess in this position, which originated with the sculptor Doi-

4. The Nike (Victory) of Samothrace. One of the most famous pieces of the Rodian art. In Louvre Museum in Paris.

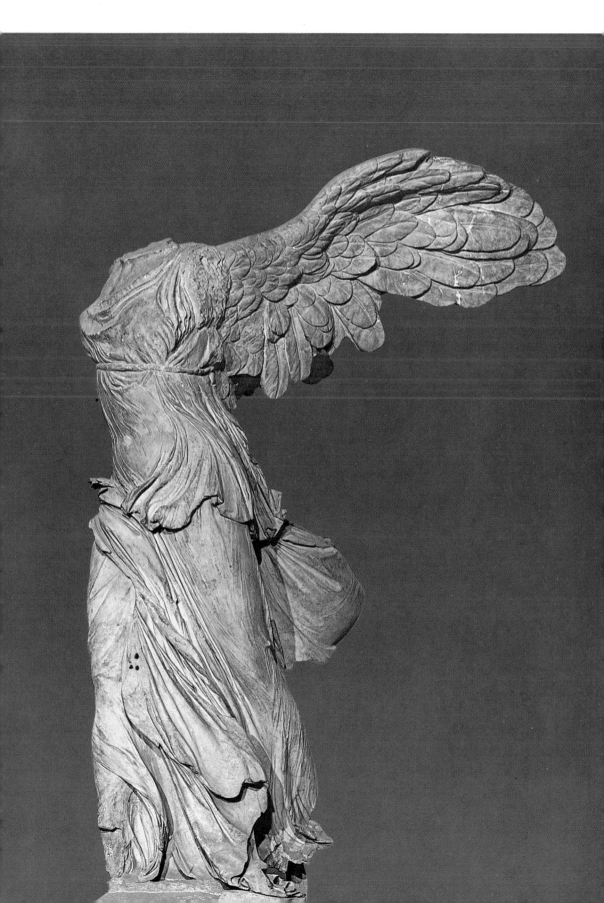

dalsas from Bithynia, another East Greek city. The main characteristic of this type is the double view we get of the figure, namely we see the torso and the lower part from different angles. This Aphrodite, a subject very popular for sculptors of the Hellenistic period, has just finished bathing and is drying her hair. Although not as magnificent as the Nike of Samothrace, this small statue (49cm) is very graceful and refined. The goddess has nothing awsome about her, nor is there explicit sensuality as in the case of other Aphrodite sculptures. One can say that it is just a pretty piece of sculpture designed to please. For this reason one can't help feeling that Greek art was reaching a dead end. Despite its beauty and grace, this work is devoid of any deeper content. It is dated to about 100 BC.

The head of Helios (Fig. 6) in the Rhodes Museum is another representative piece of the period. Some scholars think it is an imitation of the Colossus, which was destroyed in the earthquake in 227 BC. The head is 55 cm high, which means that the whole statue would have been over life-size. The face has a striking similarity to a portrait of Alexander the Great. This shows that, in the art of this period, the ideal forms of the god and the heroized human were beginning to blend. There were holes in the hair of the Helios head for insertion of golden spikes, the rays of the sun. There is a touch of sensuality in this piece, exemplified by the half-open lips, but the exreme pathos such as we have seen in the Laokoon is no longer there, and there is a tendency to return to the more serene classical Style. Once more, there is nothing awe-inspiring about the head, it is an expression of human beauty, which fails to evoke religious feelings. It is dated to the 2nd cent. BC.

Some final words about the function of sculpture: Today we tend to associate works of art with museums, art galleries and private collections. In antiquity, sculptures were primarily dedications to sanctuaries; they were often exhibited in the structures connected with the sanctuaries, like porticoes. Thus a fusion of the religious and secular aspect was effected. In the portico of Lindos, many famous works of art by important artists were exhibited. The statues represented either the deity or the portrait of the dedicator. Another area in which sculptures were exhibited was the market place where statues of eminent citizens were set up. This practice is still prevalent in our day when statues of politicans, kings, generals and poets are set up in squares. A final use was to set up a statue as a funerary monument over a tomb.

The position of the artist in the Hellenistic period varied. Many works of art have the name of the sculptor inscribed on the base, and this suggests that the artist was proud of his profession and saw himself as creative. On the other hand, artists were not the stars they are now, nor could they get away with what

5. «Aphrodite of Rhodes» (1st century BC). It is a remodelling
   of an Aphrodite by the Vithynian sculptor Diodalsa.

6. *Head of the god Helios, of marble with holes around the hairline to which the rays were attached. It was found behind the «Inn of Provence», not far from the eminence of the Castello, said to have been the site of the ancient sanctuary of Helios: (Archaeological Museum, Rhodes).*

modern artists inflict on the public of today. Ancient sculptors are often anonymous, and it seems that in these cases the artist saw himself as an executor, who just finished the job he undertook, much like a builder or a plumber does today. So the position varied according to what status the artist had really achieved.

Roman Period

In the 1st cent. BC., Augustus became emperor (or **princeps** to use a more precise term) and the Roman Republic came to an end. Rhodes was now a Roman province, but it was well treated; it became a place for political exiles. Despite the various blows delivered to her economy, Rhodes maintained a cultural prestige. Cicero and Julius Ceasar (1st cent. BC) both studied rhetoric in Rhodes. Augustus' successor, the emperor Tiberius, retired to Rhodes for a period of seclusion, before he became emperor. This means that the island was considered just as desirable a place for vacation then, as it is now.

A Roman temple on the Acropolis of Lindos testifies to the continued interest of the Romans in the island. According to the Danish scholar E. Dyggve, the temple was dedicated to the deified emperor Diocletian (3rd cent. AD).

Destructive earthquakes and raids plagued Rhodes towards the end of antiquity, in the 3rd cent. AD. In the 4th cent. AD, it became a Metropolis of Christianity with several Chistian bishops under its jurisdiction. Thus, with the introduction of Christianity as the official religion, the era of antiquity ends.

Medieval Period

In Medieval times Rhodes was part of the Byzantine Empire and was subject to raids by Persians and Arabs, who periodically invaded the Byzantine territory. From the 11th cent. AD, the West began interfering in the Byzantine areas, during the period of the Crusades.

The Crusades are an extraordinary series of holy wars in the Levant between East and West, Christianity and Islam, which began in the 11th cent. AD. and ended in the 13th. What was the real historical signifiance of this movement? It has been described as a «singular monument o human folly», whereas Voltaire, the great rationalist of 18th cent. Enlightenment, wrote that Asia Minor was a tomb of over two million Europeans. It is clear that posterity could not approve of the intentions of the crusaders to liberate the Holy lands from the Arabs. Nor can only idealistic motives be ascribed to them. Greed for money and power, a desire to loot the rich lands of the East, among which were the rich Byzantine provinces, have all been stressed as motivating factors. A modern historian, H. Trevor-Roper, has seen the Crusades as something much more than a religious movement; they were part of a process of expansion, based on over-population and new techniques: agricultural, social and military. Their results were disastrous for Byzantium, which never recovered from the 4th Crusade, during which the Venetians sacked and looted Constantinople. The Venetians plundered Rhodes as well on different occasions, whereas some legendary figures, like Richard the Lion heart of the 3rd Crusade, stopped there on his way ot the East. Again, Rhodes' geographical position made her an especially good candidate as a stop-over station.

Constantinople was sacked by the Crusaders in 1204, as mentioned above. The Greek governor of Rhodes, Leon Gavalas, made hiself independent with the consent of the Venetians and remained more —or-less independent until the Period of the Knights in the 14th cent. AD.

Period of Knights

The Order of the Knights was a quasi-religious, quasi-military order. They were Catholics and acted as a bulwark of Christianity against Moslems, especially the Turks. Since they were Catholics, they supressed the Greek Orthodox church, and conflicts around doctrinal differences were not infrequent. Still, they saved Rhodes from the Turks, who conquered Constantinople in 1453. Rhodes became the capital of a small state, of which the neigbourng islands formed a part. The Knights came from different Catholic countries, France, Italy, Germany, Spain etc., and the official languages were Latin and French, not Greek. There was a Latin archbishop, to whom the Greek bishop was responsible. The spectacular fortifications of the city of Rhodes come from the period of the Knights as well as a number of churches and buildings. In Lindos, the Government House of the Knights as well as the church of St. John were built in this period.

Turkish Period

It was during the times of Suleiman the Magnificent, when the Ottoman Empire reached its peak, that Rhodes was finally taken by the Turks (1522). The siege was spectacular and difficult, but finally the Rhodians had to capitulate. The Knights established themselves in Malta, whereas many Rhodians left with them, going to Crete.

The Turks remained in possession of the island until 1912. It was not such a bad period for Rhodes, which had some privileges: freedom of religion and immunity from the levy of children, a practice much abhorred by the Greeks, who lost their children to the Turks. The local administrator was a high member of the Greek Orthodox church. Thus, the tradition of Orthodoxy survived the various occupations. Despite some disasters (earthquakes, fires, blowing up of the church of St. John, where gun-powder was kept), it can be said that the Greeks did rather well commercially and kept up the high standard of life, which was much better than that of the Greek mainland.

Italian Period

Rhodes was taken over by the Italians in 1912, when Italian interests clashed with Turkish. They remained in possession of the island until 1943. The remnants of Italian culture are very visible in Rhodes and Kos, especially in architecture. Although the Italians engaged in a programme of Italianization of the inhabitants involving also promotion of the Italian language, they did much that has benefitted the island. In addition to public works, they conducted excavations and restorations. The restorations at Lindos have been made by Italian archaeologists. Although the results are not considered entirely successful, the restoration makes the site of Lindos attractive and comprehensible to the visitor.

Rhodes was occupied by the Germans during the Second World War and finally joined Greece in 1947, after the end of war.

THE RELIGIOUS BACKGROUND TO THE CULT OF ATHENA LINDIA:

The Olympian Gods

One of the most striking aspects of Greek religion are the twelve Olympian gods with their anthropomorphic qualities. We encounter them in art, literature and in the myths; they are important actors in the **Iliad** and the **Odyssey** of Homer. It has been thought that it was Homer, who lived in the 8th cent. BC, who gave the Olympian gods their definitive form. He had not made them up, of course, but he had given them their anthropomorphic and «civilized» qualities which make them so distinctive and so utterly Greek. Now we know that this is not entirely true. The discovery of large portions of Oriental literature has shown that anthropomorphic gods, whose pedigree and actions are often remarkably similar to the Greek ones, existed also in the Near East. Egypt was different with her theriomorphic divinities.

But if anthropomorphism is not distinctive of Greek religion, something else is. In the Near East, gods were thought to have created men out of clay to be their slaves. The creation of Adam out of earth in the Bible is a variant of this cycle of creation myths. In Greek mythology men are not created this way. Either they are autochthonous or they are made out of stones or other materials. What is more important, they do not exist in order to be the slaves of the gods. In the Orient people address their gods as «lord», implying a slave-master relationship. This undoubtedly reflects the structure of Oriental societies. In Greece, mortals address gods by their names. In the myths they quarrel with them (this happens in Mesopotamia also) and are sometimes insolent and impertinent. The relationship between mortal and god in Greece is more egalitarian than in the Orient, where gods destroy mankind periodically, either because they are angry or, sometimes, for no reason at all. The flood story, of which the Biblical account is a good example, is an ilustration of the arbitrarines of Mesopotamian gods.

Still, the Greek gods are definitely powerful. Although milder than their Oriental counter-parts, they can be terribly cruel and revengeful. Although there is no devil in the Greek pantheon, all gods had their darker sides. Either they like a mortal and help him no matter what he does, not always for an obvious reason, or they are his enemy and try to destroy him. It is the familiar sociological model of the in -group/out-group mentality. Athena will serve as a good example of loyalty to her friends and ruthlessness to her enemies. In the Homeric poems she is the costant helper and adviser to the Greeks: Odysseus, Diomedes, Achilles. But when the Trojans, who also worship her but are the enemies of the Greeks, ask her help and bring a new garment in her temple laying it on her cult-image, she will not listen to their prayer, nor will she help. Why? It is not because the Trojans have committed a crime, but she is the friend of the Greeks at the time and that is that.

The most important distinction between mortal and god for the Greeks was that humans must die, whereas the gods live forever. For the rest there were no great differences between men and gods, in actions, moral principles or appearance. In time, however, Greek religion underwent an evolution. Many intellectuals in the 5th cent. BC no longer believed in the Olympian gods or any rational gods at all. They questioned traditional morality and religion and saw everything in terms of chance. On the other hand, some of the most eminent personalities, like Aeschylus, Sophocles and Herodotus, had a firm belief in the gods. But their beliefs had a deeper philosophical and ethical content. The expression «the divine» is often used and there is explicit or implicit belief in divine justice. Thus, from the Classical period onwards there were many ways open, ranging from the popular beliefs in the gods, as expressed by Homer, to complete atheism. The situation became more complex with the introduction of Oriental cults in later times. Still, the Olympian gods remained the basis of official Greek religion until the advent of Christianity.

Athena: Athena is an old goddess. She did not arrive together with the Dorians in the 11th cent. BC but existed already in Mycenaean times. Undoubtedly her function changed with time, however. Originally she may have been the goddess protecting the Mycenaean citadels and palaces, a hypothesis which is reinforced by the discovery of a fresco depicting a war goddess flanked by shields in the citadel of Mycenae.

In Homer, where a world of heroes is described in a legendary era before the formation of the city states, Athena is the special protectress of the Greek heroes. For this reason also, it has been assumed that in Mycenaean times Athena was the goddess of the palaces and their kings.

But after the formation of the city states as political centres (7th cent. BC), Athena became the protectres of the city. This is why she is armed and functions as a war goddess. When the Lindians were besieged by the Persians, Athena helped her people, and the Persians had to leave. She was always caled upon to help when her cities were in danger. There was another war god, Ares. but whereas the latter is bloodthirsty and personifies the violence of war, Athena is a protectres of order and the household in the city. Her war-like aspects are related to defense and protection, not agression. Armed goddesses exist also in the Orient and some aspects of Athena may have been borrowed from there.

Her other main function was patronage of the arts and crafts. In this capacity she shared a temple with another god with similar interest, Hephaestus. Their joint temple was erected above the market place in Athens. It is especially household crafts that Athena was patronizing, spinning, weaving etc. In Homer, she teaches young girls how to weave, but according to a myth she was not pleased if any mortal excelled in the art. A young girl, Arachne (spider), boasted that she was better at weaving than the goddess, and she was punished by being turned into a spider condemned to perpetual weaving of fragile threads. The myth demonstrates the cruel side of divinity of which something has been said above.

Although these feminine tasks were Athena's specialty, she also protected the goldsmith, the potter etc. For this reason she attracted the lower classes, and she represented the vital functions of the city state. She was the city-godess **par excellence,** exemplifying the most characteristic aspects of civilization: order and industrial production. This embodiment of civilization, which Athena represents can be deduced from the following myth. Athena and Poseidon wanted both to be the protectors of Athens, and competed in producing items that would be most desirable to the Athenians. Poseidon's gift was a spring of salt-water or a horse, Athena's an olive tree. The Athenians chose Athena's gifts but when Poseidon got angry, they worshipped him also on the Acropolis. This is a local Attic legend, which was also depicted on the West pediment of the Parthenon on the Acropolis. What does it tell us about Athena? There is clearly a conflict in the centre of the myth, and the opposition between the two gods is expressed by the nature of their gifts. Nature and violence are the essence of Poseidon's gifts. The salt water, the sea, is a source of livelihood but also of danger. The horse is very usefull to man but typical of aggression and war. Athena's olive tree symbolizes peaceful occupations: cultivation of the earth and making of oil. In Poseidon offers the sea, Athena offers the wood to make ships.

So far I have stressed Athena as a goddess of the city **par excellence.** Some of the myths surrounding her, however, as well as some of her attributes reveal some other aspects. First her birth. She was not born in the normal way but sprang from the head of her father, Zeus, who had swallowed her mother. When Athena was due to be born, Zeus got a terrible headache and asked Hephaestus to split his head with an axe. Hephaestus was afraid, but he finally obeyed the orders. When he struck Zeus' head, Athena sprang forth fully armed. The myth expresses the special relationship Athena had with her father, and places her high in the rank of Olympian deities. On the other hand, the manner of her birth (depicted in the east pediment of the Parthenon) conceals a certain violence. Th splitting of the head with an axe is deadly under normal circumstances, but Zeus, being immortal, survives it.

Another myth also has to do with violence. A characteristic piece of equipment of Athena, through which we can always recognize her in art, is the Aegis. This is a goat skin, to which the head of the monster Medusa was attached.

Medusa or Gorgon was so terrifying, that anyone who looked at it was turned into stone. It had snakes instead of hair, which enhanced the horror. The most wide-spread version of the myth relating to the Gorgon head says that it was given to her by a hero, Perseus, who slew the monster. But another myth says that the monster was called Pallas and was Athena's own father, whom she killed and then got dressed in the skin. Thus, we have two myths of completely different content, which express a relationship of violence between Athena and her father, whether he be Zeus or the monstrous Pallas. Perhaps their message is hostility to the male sex. Athena remained a virgin, and one cannot help feeling that a deeper conflict between the sexes is expressed here. To this the above mentioned story with Poseidon lends some support, because Poseidon is also an old god, related to fertlity.

Despite her virginity, Athena is female, and it is natural that she would attract female worshippers in the cities, in which she was a patron goddess. Thus, both in Athens and in Lindos she had a special relation with women, either helping young virgins, like herself, or mothers to be. Some fertility rituals, the Arrhephoria, were celebrated in Athens in connection with her cult.

In summary, Athena embodies many aspects, some of which are civilized and some of which look very primitive. This is explicable given her ancient origin and the fact that she may have absorbed local goddesses. It should be also kept in mind that the cult varied from place to place. In Lindos, for example, there was a peculiarity in the cult of Athena, about which more will be said further on.

Sanctuary: Sanctuary is a term designating a holy place. Greek sanctuaries could be built in the city or in the country, on top of a mountain or next to a gorge. Landscape was definitely a factor which influenced the choice of the spot as anyone who has visited Delphi, or Lindos will have observed.

Temenos: Greek sanctuaries include the following elements: 1. **Temenos. This is the ground of the sanctuary.** It always has definite boundaries, usually a wall 2m high, but it is accessible to all. This contrasts greatly with the Orient. In Egypt, the great sanctuaries were surrounded by massive walls which gave an impression of a fortress. Similarly, in Mesopotamia, temples were inaccessible and were often placed on top of plattforms imitating mountains. Only the priests had free access to the sacred grounds in the Orient, and they were an exclusive and priviledged class. In Greece, priests were ordinary members of the community serving a term of office. The temenos was accessible to all citizens not to priests alone.

Altar: Inside the temenos, with its definite boundaries, there was a temple and an altar. The altar was a very essential element of the sanctuary: all sanctuaries had altars but not all of them had temples. The altar could vary in form, ranging from an elaborately built structure to a natural formation, such as rock. It all depended on the wealth and position of the sanctuary. Some altars were formed by the accumulation of ash and burned animal bones, or even animal horns. **The standard altar was built with rectangular blocks and was often whitewashed. On top of it, a fire was burning for the sacrificial victims to be**

28

burned. The altar stood in front of the temple, so that the temple façade formed a scenic backdrop for the main cult activity: sacrifice. The sacrifices and prayers were performed at the altar and outside the temple. In some cases the temenos included tiers arranged in a theatrical way for the spectators partaking in the ritual. More will be said further on about the similarity of ritual to drama.

When an animal was sacrificed, its entrails, fat and bones were placed on the altar and burned, an offering to the gods, while the flesh was cooked and eaten by the participants.

According to the Danish excavator Chr. Blinkenberg, the temenos of Athena Lindia did not contain an altar, nor was animal sacrifice performed. Only bloodless offerings were given to the goddess. This is an extremely unlikely hypothesis, however, as we will see below.

Temple: The temple was regarded as the house of the deity and housed the cult image. The very first temples, around the 9th cent. BC, were long buildings; some contained benches and a hearth for the cooking of common meals to be eaten under the auspices of the gods. This latter type of building should perhaps not be called a temple at all but rather sacred «banquetting house». Later, the canonical form of the temple developped. An oblong, rectangular building with a cult image inside and an altar outside. Columns were placed on the outside to support the roof, thus forming a portico. This was a crucial architectural element which gave the Greek temple its distinctive appearance especially when compared with the Egyptian ones.

In Egypt the columns were placed inside and they formed huge pillar halls creating the effect of a forest of columns. The psychological impact was one of awe and magnificence, and it was definitely overwhelming. The Greeks chose to place the pillars outside the temple, either along the short walls only (as is the case with the temple of Athena Lindia), or along all four sides. The effect was the opposite of what I have described about Egypt. The columns outside give an illusion of transparent walls through which the light can move freely, and the whole structure is lightened. Greek temples do not make an impact by their mass but rather through grace and the geometrical sense of form and proportions. The number of columns was always carefully chosen in relation to the length and width of the temple. It can be shown that the architects had worked out the proportions carefully «on paper», applying mathematical principles, before they got to the actual building of the temple.

The temple of Athena Lindia, which we see today, was built in the 4th cent. BC. It conformed to a standard plan, having three rooms in a row along the axis: an anteroom, the cella, where the cult image was placed, and a backroom used for different purposes, such as storage. The Greek terms for these three rooms are **pronaos, naos, opisthodomos.** It had columns along the short sides.

Cult Images: The architecture of the temple was, to a great extent, dictated by the need to display the cult image. The latter was placed against the cella wall so that it would be visible even from the outside, provided the temple door was open, and that the spectator stood along the axis. When ceremonies took place at the altar, the cult image would be visible, and the deity would thus take part in the ceremony.

Early cult images were made out of wood and were often reputed to have fallen from the sky, which testifies to their great antiquity. Some cult images may have survived from Mycenaean times. The Greeks called them **xoana.** We know very little about their appearance, since none have survived, but it is very probable that they were «abstract» and not fully anthropomorphic.

In the 8th cent. BC., the period we have called the «Greek Renaissance», a new type developed made out of wood, bronze or clay. These cult images were made for new temples, which were founded in this period in great numbers, and the god or goddess was seated. Such was the type of the cult image of Athena Lindia made for her first temple in the 8th cent. This image was burned in the 4th cent. A new temple was then built, and a new cult image was made, probably influenced by the Pheidian one in the Parthenon. The cult images of the Classical period (5th and 4th centuries BC) were fully anthropomorphic. Pheidias made a great impact, first by his creation of the image of Zeus at Olympia, which was huge and made out of gold and ivory, and then by that of Athena in the Parthenon, also made out of these materials. The latter was standing and definitely over life-size, reaching almost to the ceiling.

The cult image was the personification of the god. The more ancient the cult image, the more sacred it was considered. Th protective power of Athena, for example, was thought to reside in her old cult image, the **palladion** as it was called. It is interesting that, although the Athenians of the 5th cent. BC spent a tremendous amount of money on the Pheidian cult image made out of precious materials, they worshipped the old cult image which was housed, not in the Parthenon, but in the Erechtheion. This is where the new garment, woven by the young girls of Athens, was brought. The ancients spoke of the Pheidian sculpture in terms of its beauty and its value in money. In this way the Parthenon of Athens was more of a display of Athenian culture and wealth than a centre of worship.

The temple of Athena on the rock of the acropolis of Lindos.

The Sanctuary of Athena Lindia

History of excavation: Excavations at the Acropolis of Lindos were begun systematically by the Danish archaeologists K.F. Kinch and Chr. Blinkengerg. Their results were published in six volumes published by the «Fondation Carlesberg» of Denmark. The first two volumes (1931) deal with the objects, the nect two (1941) with inscriptions. All four are written by Blinkenberg. The architecture was published much later, in 1960, in two volumes, by E. Dyggve who disagrees with many of the conclusions drawn by Blinkenberg.

In 1910-1916 and 1929-1932 the Italian archaeologists Maiuri and Jacopi worked on the site. It should be noted that the island was under Italian occupation at the time, and the Italians took an interest in the antiquities. They are responsible for the restoration of the antiquities of Lindos which contribute to the popularity of the site today.

The Cult of Lindos. The word Lindia (of Lindos), which is a constant epithet of the goddess, is of non-Greek origin etymologically. Therefore, it seems that a cult existed in Lindos long before the Greeks, perhaps even before the Mycenaeans, who were Greek-speaking. When the Dorians brought their goddess Athena with them, she was assimilated with the older goddess, a phenomenon which is very common in the history of religion. For example, Athena of antiquity has now been assimilated to Virgin Mary (Panaghia), whose church is to be seen in the village. According to Dyggve, even the temple of Athena Lindia was turned into a church fo Virgin Mary in the Christian era.

Apart from the name, another detail points to an older, pre-existing cult in Lindos before Athena's arrival. This detail comes from a poem by the 5th-cent. poet Pindar, who gives the following mythical account of the establishment of Athena's cult: Zeus had a terrible head-ache and asked Hephaestus to split his head. Hephaestus struck with a brazen hatchet and Athena lept forth from her father's head and cried aloud with a mighty shout, while Heaven and Mother Earth trembled before her. Then the Sun god, who brings light to men, asked his dear children to be the first to build an altar for the new goddess and, by founding a holy sacrifice, to gladden the heart of the father and daughter. But sometimes mortals are driven from the right path, and they forgot to take fire with them. So they performed the sacred rite without fire in the grove of the Acropolis... (Olympian VII, 35-49).

This is clearly a myth designed to explain a ritual, namely the custom of performing fireless rites in connection with the cult of Athena Lindia. This deviated from standard Greek practice, which demanded fire on the altar and burning of the entrails of the sacrificial victims. This deviation from standard practice can be explained, if the cult of Athena was assimilated to an older cult.

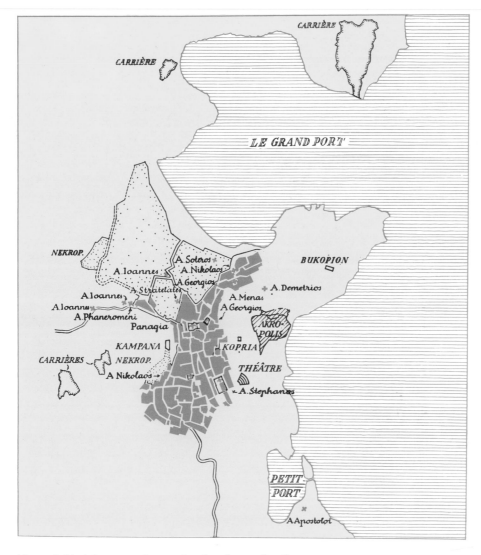

Map of Lindo's area, the ports, the Acropolis, the monuments and the village.

Blinkenberg suggested that no sacrifice was performed at all in the sanctuary, and that only fruits of the earth, bloodless offerings, were made. He also stressed that there was no altar. He concluded that the prehistoric goddess, venerated before Athena, was a vegetation goddess, who did not require animal sacrifice.

Blinkenberg's hypothesis has found general acceptance, but it may need modification. First, Dyggve identified architectural evidence of an altar. Second and most important, there is archaeological evidence of animal bones and ashes from the temenos area outside the temple. Third, votive animal figurines, as well as

33

figurines of men carrying aminals, have been found. All this suggests that animals were sacrificed. Blinkenberg himself was puzzled by the remnants of animal bones and ashes, but he explained them as remnants of sacred banquets, which took place in connection with the cult. This makes sense, but it is difficult to accept that the killing and cooking of the animals was a ceremony quite separate from the offering ritual.

What is the solution? Can Pindar's testimony be ignored? Perhaps a close reading of the text will give a clue. Pindar says that the sons of the Sun god forgot to take fire with them. Their intention, however, was to perform sacrifice, and Pindar does not say that they did not perform it; he says that they performed rites **without** fire. Perhaps the solution is that they performed the sacrifice and ate the meat but did not burn the entrails. This would deviate from standard Greek practice (for sacrificial ritual, see further on) but would allow the killing of the animal and the eating of the meat by the participants, a practice which had a very important social function. This is only a hypothesis, but it reconciles the Pindaric account with the archaeological evidence.

A different solution has been suggested, Pidar's poem does not refer to Lindos at all but some other city on Rhodes. The wording of the lines, however, do not suport this supposition. Pindar mentions other cities, but Lindos is mentioned last and the next line begins with «there it is that...». Thus, the Pindaric account has to be taken as serious evidence for the cult, whatever interpretation we give to it.

The Temple Chronicle and the Epiphanies of the goddess:
In the area of Hagios Stephanos (see map), a marble stele was found with valuable inscription concerning the history of the temple and with a list of offerings through the ages. This is the Temple Chronicle, composed in the 1st cent. BC. It was compiled by a certain Timachidas, and its purpose was to advertise the wealth and importance of the sanctuary.

For us it is valuable as a source of religious belief in the Hellenistic period and as a historical source. Among the most interesting accounts of the Temple Chronicle are the Epiphanies (appearances) of Athena to mortals.

Although Athena can appear in person in the Homeric poems, in the historical period she appeared in men's dreams. Such forms of epiphany were common in antiquity, and some Greek sanctuaries, like that of Asclepius at Epidaurus, had special arrangements for people to sleep in the hope that the god would visit them at night.

One epiphany of Athena occurred at the time of the Persian invasion in 490:

"When Darius, King of Persia, sent forth a great army for the purpose of enslaving Hellas, this island was the first which his fleet visited. The people in the country were terrified at the approach of the Persians and fled for safety to all the strongholds, most of them gathering at Lindus. Thereupon the barbarians set about to besiege them, until the Lindians, sore-pressed by a water shortage, were

34

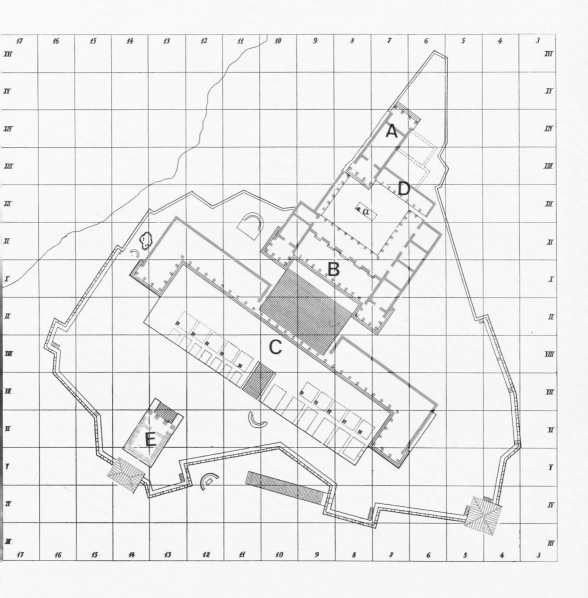

*Plan of Acropolis after Dyggve: A. The temple of Lindian Athe-
na. B. The Propylaia. C. The Grand Stoa. D. The Ionic Stoa. E.
Temple of the deified emperor Diocletian. 3rd cent AD.*

minded to hand over the city to the enemy. Right at this juncture the goddess stood over one of the magistrates in his sleep and bade him be of good courage, since she herself would procure, by intercession with her father, the water they needed. The one who saw the vision rehearsed to the citizens Athena's command. So they investigated and found that they had only enough water to last for five days, and accordingly they asked the barbarians for a truce for just that number of days, saying that Athena had sent to her father for help, and that if help did not come in the specified time, they would surrender the city. When Datis, the admiral of Darius, heard this request, he immediately burst out laughing. But the next day, when a great cloud gathered about the Acropolis and a heavy shower fell inside the cloud, so that contrary to all expectations (paradoxos) the besieged had plenty of water, while the Persian army suffered for lack of it, the barbarian was struck by the epiphany of the goddess. He took off his personal adornment and sent it as an offering —his mantle, his necklace, and his bracelets, and in addition his tiara, his scimitar, and even his chariot, which formerly was preserved here, but was burned along with most of the offerings when the priest of Helios was Eucles, son of Astyanactidas (probably soon after 350 B.C.), when the temple caught fire. As for Datis, he set forth on the business before him, after establishing peace with the besieged and declaring publicly, "These men are protected by the gods".

(From F.G. Grant, Hellenistic Religions, New York 1953)

In this account Athena lives up to her reputation as a protectress of her city. It is very interesting that the Christian God performed a similar miracle in the reign of the Roman emperor Marcus Aurelius in the 2nd cent. AD. He sent a violent rain which drowned the enemy but quenched the thirst of the Roman soldiers, some of which were Christians and had prayed to their God.

The History of the Temple and Cult Image:
Blinkenberg reconstructs the history of the temple as follows. At first there was no temple structure at all, only a grove to which Pindar refers also. The first structure may have been built in the 6th cent. BC. We do not know this; we can infer it only by analogy from other sites.

A better temple must have been built by the tyrant Kleoboulos in the 6th cent. BC. He may also have strengthened the cult of the goddess, as other tyrants did with local gods of their city-states, in an attempt to foster national-religious feeling. We know that Peisistratus strengthened the cult of Athena at Athens and Polycrates built a magnificent temple to Hera on Samos. Tyrants had also another reason for building temples: They absorbed the unemployed. The promotion of national religion strengthened the political base of the tyrant's power.

36

7. *Figurine possibly representing Athena Lindia.*

7. *Varvakeios Athena, a copy of Pheidias' statue.*

The cult image of this temple has naturally been lost, but Blinkenberg reconstructs it as a seated figure with a special hat (polos) wearing necklaces and other jewelry. He infers that from votive figurines of terracotta found in the sanctuary of a colony of Lindos which may reproduce the statue. (Fig. **7**)

At the time of Kleoboulos there was also an impressive stairway, 7,5m. broad, which led up to the temple and was used for processions. This stairway went through an enclosure wall which marked off the temenos from the rest of the Acropolis. The first built altar was probably erected then. An interesting detail: the Kleoboulos temple was built above a natural cave in the cliff, which cave must have been a cult place in prehistoric times. It was perhpas the cave which dictated the choice of spot for the temple at the very edge of the cliff. In Byzantine times, this cave was used for the worship of Virgin Mary.

4th cent. B.C.: Around 342, the Kleoboulos temple was burned, and a new one was built in its place in the end of the 4th cent. or around 300 BC. The whole temenos area was later reorganized, the most important addition being the Propylaea, an elaborate gate-structure leading to the temenos.

The new temple was in the Doric order. It had three rooms and two rows of four columns, along the short sides. (The terminus technicus is amphiprostylos). Its dimensions were 7.75 X 21.65 m.

A new cult image was created for the new temple, the type of which we can infer, once more, from votive terracotta figurines. The goddess was represented
standing and carrying a shield, and the statue almost certainly reflects Pheidian
style and the Athena of the Parthenon at Athens. But on her head she did not
wear a helmet, like the Athenian one, but a polos hat, like that of the older cult
image. An inscription makes some reference to jewelry, so it is quite possible that
this image also was ornated with pectorals and necklaces. The Temple Chronicle
of Lindos gives us some additional information. The statue was fastened against
the short wall of the cella, thus facing the spectator as he entered from the door.
Why was it fastened? Perhaps it was necessary to secure it in position if it were
too big to balance itself effectively on its own weight, especially since there was
always fear of earthquakes. It must have been over lifesize. The materials could
have been wood for the main body and ivory for the extremities, feet, arms, head.
The Lindians could not have afforded a gold and ivory statue as the Athenians
did.

The fame of the temple can be deduced from the fact that Alexander the Great
and many of his successors offered magnificent sacrifices there, and dedicated
weapons after victories. It can also be inferred from the quality of votive gifts,
many of which were famous in antiquity and are mentioned in the Temple Chronicle. The sculptor Boethus, the painter Parrhasios of Ephesos and other great
artists had their works exibited in the sanctuary.

Propylaea: The Propylaea were built in the first half of the 3rd cent. BC. and
this involved a radical change in the appearance of the sanctuary. Before, the temenos was marked off by a low wall, now this low wall was replaced by the
monumental façade of the Propylaea to which a very broad stairway gave access.
(fig.8) The Propylaea were in the Doric order and were Π-shaped. The emphasis
was on the wings, which looked like the façades of the temple. In this way the
temple façade is anticipated before the visitor enters the temenos. The arrange-
ment was designed to direct the visitor through a series of surprises and chan-
ging views and to prepare him for a crescendo upon reaching the temenos. We
must imagine that the view changed constantly with gradual ascent by the staircase. When the visitor reached the top, he had to pass through a hall, which was
bordered by columns on the long sides. He was then confronted with a spectacular panoramic view on the one hand, on the other he could see the temple
against this view. The temple was off the main axis, but the altar stood in the
centre of the temenos. This was the sacrificial altar, identified by Dyggve. Another
one, smaller, and destined for bloodless offerings, was placed inside the temple
in front of the cult image.

The Propylaea were asymmetrical, but his could be seen only from the inside;
from the outside they gave the illusion of complete symmetry. The rooms of the

38

8. Reconstruction of the Propylaia after Dyggve.

wings (Fig. 9) were designed for banquetting which followed the sacrifice and for display of the most spectacular votive offerings, the greatest works of art. But the main function of the whole structure was to isolate the temenos and to screen off unpurified visitors.

The following prohibitions were effective regarding entrance to the sanctuary: Carrying weapons was prohibited. One had to be decently dressed with the head covered. One had to be barefoot or else wear white shoes, which could **not** be made out of horse's skin. You could not enter at all immediately after loss of virginity; after an abortion; during menstruation; after you had come into contact with a dead body; after intercourse, unless a purification bath had taken place, etc. These instructions shed light on the notions of impurity of the ancients.

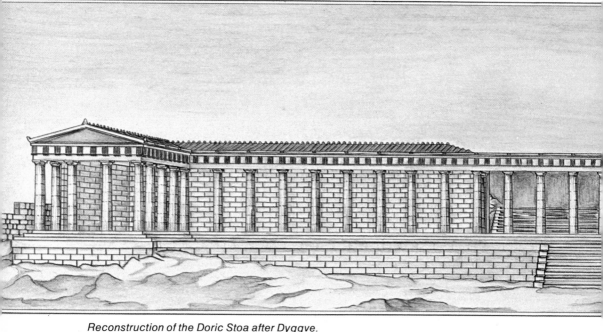

Reconstruction of the Doric Stoa after Dyggve.

The Portico end of 3rd cent.: The Hellenistic period was one of artistic exaggeration. If the early art of the Greeks is characterized by modesty and simplicity, the late art and architecture, during the Hellenistic period, delights in dramatic effect. We have seen this in art (compare the Krito-Timaresta relief with the Laokoon, (Fig.1,3) and it is valid for architecture as well. By the end of the 3rd cent., the monumental Propylaea were no longer considered magnificent enough in themselves, and another structure had to be added to enhance dramatic effect. This structure was a **Doric portico or stoa** which duplicated the façade of the Propylaea but on a much larger scale. The main difference in plan was the complete symmetry of the Portico. The element of surprise, which was the principle of the architects of the Propylaea, was repeated here as well. Most important must have been the interplay of light and shade, as one passed from the staircase to the columns of the central part. The centre of the long side of the Portico was cut by the stairway which led up to the Propylaea. In a way the Portico was built as an entrance to this stairway, just as the Propylaea were built as an entrance to the temenos. The experience was thus repeated twice, and the visitor's expectations were rising with each ascent.

It is with purpose that the wings of the Portico reproduce the façade of the temple, as was the case in the Propylaea. The temple was, after all, the emblem of the sanctuary and the culmination of the experience.

The function of the Portico was more secular. It was outside the temenos and served as an art gallery and as a shady area, much needed during the hot summer days.

Later Structures: Later additions destroyed rather than enhanced the effect. The terrace was enlarged in the 1st cent. BC. Beneath this terrace there were 10 vaulted cisterns for the collection of water. In the 2nd cent. AD an **Ionic portico** was added in the temenos area, thus blocking the dramatic landscape which acted as a backdrop to the temenos. Finally, the view from the other side of the acropolis was blocked by the erection of a **Roman temple** in the 3rd cent. AD, presumably for the cult of a deified emperor. Some think it was for the cult of the hero Psithyros.

Votive Offerings: In our times, it is often the case that votives are placed on an icon of the Greek Orthodox Church as tokens of gratitude for a difficulty or illness which has been overcome. These offerings are jewelry or silver/gold limbs

41

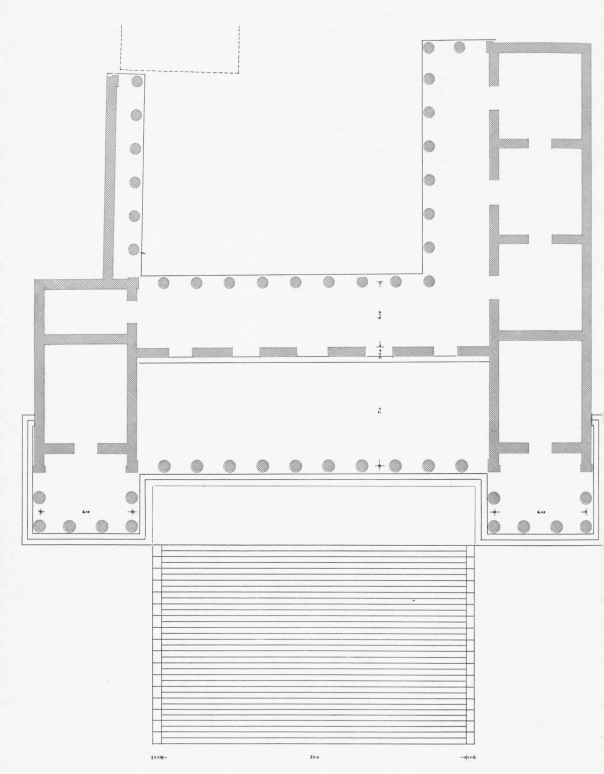

9. Plan of a section of the Propylaia (gate) showing the stairway, the porticoes and the various rooms. The rooms on the right were used for banquetting. Reconstruction after Dyggve.

representing the healed parts of the body. Ancient offerings were even more varied. Their value depended on the economic status of the dedicator. They could range from large-scale sculptures in stone, or bronze, to small figurines. They could be jewelry, vases, weapons, and objects of every-day use such as mirrors and spindlewhirls. Most often they had the form of terracotta figurines representing humans or animals. Sometimes the cult image of the divinity was represented, but more frequently it was the mortal who presented himself as an adorant and servant to the god.

In the sanctuary of Athena Lindia figurines of musicians, horsemen, men carrying animals (for sacrifice) have been found, representing different categories of worshippers. It is female figurines that predominate, however, because of Athena's special relationship with women as a protectress of the household. Mothers holding a child are frequently represented; they were placing the child under the protection of Athena. A special type is the seated boy, which is attested also in Cyprus. Were these boys rendering services to the temple for a period and do the figurines symbolize this? if so, we have an Oriental custom here. There is also a type of male figurine reclining and holding a drinking vessel. This must allude to the sacrificial banquetting which took place in the rooms of the Propylaea. Exotic animals like lions as well as birds and cats are suggestive of the power of Athena over nature. There are also objects brought from abroad, gifts from foreigners who visited the sanctuary. Egyptian, Near Eastern and Cypriot objects are attested in significant quantities. A final category of objects represents cult implements: Lamps and torches used in processions, baskets which would be filled with fruit and offered, wine jars and drinking cups which are related to the feasting.

Cult of Zeus Polieus

Blinkenberg thought that, in the Hellenistic, period the cult of Zeus Polieus (patron of the city) was added to that of Athena, and that they shared the same temple. He bases this assumption on epigraphic evidence, namely a dedicatory formula saying: «To Athena Polias and to Zeus Polieus». This assumption cannot be proven but let it be said that it was not unusual for Greek deities to share temples. Athena shared the Hephaisteion temple in Athens with Hephaistus, while she shared the Erechtheion on the Acropolis with Poseidon and others.

Sacrificial Ritual and the Boukopion of Lindos

On the NE side of the Acropolis of Lindos, there is a sanctuary by the name of Boukopion which will be more fully described later. It was used for animal sacrifices, and that is exactly what Bou-kopion means: slaughtering-place of bulls. The Danish excavator Chr. Blinkenberg, who believed that animal sacrifice could **not** be performed in the sanctuary of Athena Lindia on the Acropolis, suggested that the Boukopion was built expressly for fulfilling the need for sacrifice. But why was sacrificial ritual necessary? Blinkenberg was right in stressing its importance, since there are very few Greek cults from which animal sacrifice is missing. Morover, animal sacrifice is part of the canonical, established cult pattern for the Olympian gods. Thus, Blinkenberg reasoned, if the Lindians could not sacrifice to Athena on the Acropolis because the traditions of the older cult were very strong still and forbade the practice, they could at least sacrifice in the Boukopion outside the Acropolis.

Blinkenberg's hypothesis about the absence of animal sacrifice on the Acropolis may not be correct, as we have seen, especially since another Danish archaeologist, E. Dyggve, identified traces of a sacrificial altar. However, he was probably right to some extent; animal sacrifice on the Acropolis involved some **abnormality, since no fire was used.** About this the testimony of the poet Pindar is unmistakable. Thus, we can agree with Blinkenberg that in the Boukopion the necessary conditions for normal sacrificial ritual were fulfilled.

One of the most striking aspects of Greek religion is the amount of animal blood shed in the names of the gods. So central is sacrifice in Greek cult practices, that an ingenious theory has been proposed, tracing back the origin of this practice to Palaeolithic times and relating it to hunting ritual. Since hunting was essential for the existence of early man, and since 97% of man's total history evolves in the Palaeolothic period, hunting never ceased to play an important role even with the advent of cililization.

Sacrifice appeals to some of man's most deeply rooted instincts: The sight of blood evokes horror and fear of death. The meal that follows provides appeasement of hunger and reinforcement of social solidarity. In short, sacrifice operates on many levels, social and psychological. It fulfills the hunting instinct in a way which is not detrimental to the welfare of the community. Food is provided and hierarchy of roles is reinforced, since ritual is by nature very structured.

A few words will be said about the structure of sacrificial ritual.

1. The priests, who are going to perform the ceremony, undergo a special preparation. They purify themselves by bathing and adorn themselves. The animal also may be specially adorned, for example its horns may be guilded. This preparation stage marks the beginning of the ceremony and the «sacrilization» stage.

General view of the acropolis of Lindos with the village and the harbour.

2. The animal is led to the altar. A basket is brought into which the sacrificial knife is hidden beneath corn, fruit and/or cakes. Music is played.

3. The participants stand around the altar, which is situated in front of the temple. They take corn from the basket and throw it at the animal. The priest says a prayer.

4. The knife, the instrument of death, is revealed from the basket. Some hair from the animal is cut and thrown in the fire of the altar.

5. The actual killing follows. Smaller animals are held above the altar, while their throat is slit. Large animals are stunned first, and then their throat is slit. The women utter a cry at the moment of death. This marks the climax of the action.

Lindos: entrance to the acropolis.

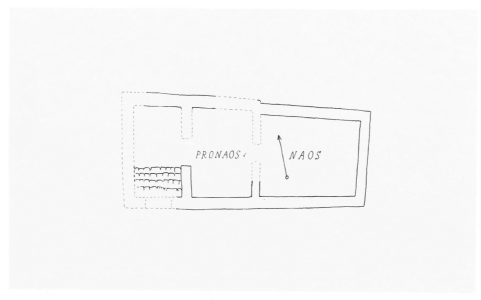

12. Plan of the Boukopion temple. After Dyggve.

6. The animal is skinned. Its bones, fat and entrails are burned on the altar, whereas the meat is distributed to the participants. The feasting often took place right in the sanctuary. In Lindos it took place in the rooms of the Propylaea.

Other types of sacrifice exist also. What has just been described is the normal type of sacrifice for the Olympian gods. A slightly different procedure was followed for the deities of the underworld and for the heroes.

The ritual was higly structured like a Greek tragedy. Like a drama, it leads the participant through stages which are increasingly charged with tension and emotional excitement, until the climax is reached with the killing of the animal. For example, anticipation for the killing is aroused by the cutting of the animal's hair or with the revelation of the knife, which is hidden in the basket. The cry of the women, when the animal is struck, express anxiety about death, but at the same time it releases tension.

Sacrifice is not only a central ritual in the practice of Greek religion but a frequent theme in Greek myths. Not only does animal sacrifice occur but sacrifice of virgins (Iphigeneia) or children (Medea's children, Thyestes myth etc.). The preoccupation with sacrifice is a feature, which the student of Greek religion has to study seriously. When the visitor views the white temples and marbles of ancient Greece, he suspects very little about the cult practices, which went together with them.

The Site

Visit to Lindos: Lindos lies 55 km to the S. of the city of Rhodos and is accessible by bus or even by small boats during the summer season. The trip by car takes a little less than an hour and the road is very good. For this reason one can even rent a car and drive without being apprehensive about the possible misfortunes due to the conditions of some Greek roads.

When you come close to Lindos, there is a long beach, Vlechá, to your left or N. of the Acropolis which towers over the landscape. On this beach, there exists the only major hotel of Lindos, Rhodos Bay Hotel. Otherwise, accommodations can be found in the village: there are rooms to let in pensions or private houses.

The bus, or car, has to stop in the square of the village; from there one has to go on foot because the village streets are too narrow. The square is well equipped for the tourist: you can buy film, souvenirs, refreshments, and there are restaurants as well.

Partial view of the village of Lindos with the Acropolis in the background.

Pictoresque, cobbled street.

The Village: The village is one of the most picturesque ones in Rhodes, retaining a lot of the original island architecture through the ages. The houses are built on different levels and are all whitewashed. Some of them are very old, dating from the time of the Knights, and have a very impressive façade with emblems of eagles or a cross in relief above the door. The visitor must be warned to wear flat shoes in the village, because the streets are cobbled, and shoes with high heels make for very unpleasant walking.

The houses conform to a basic plan. Behind the door which faces the street, there is always a court, paved in a special mosaic technique with black and white pebbles. Around this court, the rooms of the house are arranged. Thus, the rooms do not normally connect with one another but communicate only through the court. Sometimes there is an upper storey.

The little harbour of St. Paul.

The most spacious and elaborate room, corresponding to our living-room, is called «to kaló spiti», the «special room». This is reserved for the entertainment of guests and is always kept clean and nice. In order to keep it clean, the lady of the house has all the furniture covered with sheets to protect them from the dust, and the result is that the family itself never enjoys it. It is a display and status room for the outsiders. This mentality is not unique for the Lindians but is shared by most Greeks as well. The «special room» is nicely paved and normally includes a large vault, which is another architectural feature of Lindian architecture. In smaller houses the special room has a raised platform along one of its walls, where the newly-wed couple sleep.

The other rooms are the kitchen with a baking oven, the WC etc. In some cases a charming mixture of modernity and tradition is effected. The original arran-

Entrance to the harbour of St. Paul with the church of the Apostles.

gement of the rooms around the court is kept, but the rooms are connected with each other. The old paved floors have been replaced by wooden ones and the walls are not covered with embroideries but modern prints. The TV set is hardly missing from any house nowadays, while the kitchen would compete with any European one in the latest models of equipment.

The village is full of tourist shops. The special products are embroideries and the famous Lindian ceramics.

The ceramics, mostly in the form of plates, (Fig.10) are characterized by polychrome motifs. They flourished in the 16th-17th centuries, and they were so much appreciated, that they travelled all over the world. Specimens of old Lindian plates can be seen in Lindos, the Museum of Rhodes, the Benaki Museum in Athens, but the largest collection exists in the Cluny Museum, Paris.

Although we speak of «Lindian» plates, there is, in fact, quite a controversy about their origin. According to one story, the art of these ceramics was introduced to Lindos by Persian artists who had been captured by the Knights. Another tradition makes the Great Master of the Knights, H. de Villeneuve, a patron of this art, and he may have introduced artists from the East to teach the Lindians. Finally, some believe that the plates were not manufactured in Lindos at all, but in some cities of N. Asia Minor. In this view Rhodes acted only as a transit station for their distribution further west and thus got the reputation for their manufacture.

Whatever the truth, it is clear that the tradition points to the East. In addition, the motives and the technique are undeniably Eastern. Birds, antithetical animals, floral motifs, etc., have a remarkably long tradition in the East. Antithetical animals, for example, are attested in Mesopotamia since the 3rd millennium BC. The persistence of the tradition is a good reminder of the continuity of civilization. This becomes even more apparent if one compares pottery from 7th cent. BC Greece with some Lindian plates of the 17th cent. AD. Both have filling ornaments, both use versions of the spiral motif, in both the surface is completely covered. There is a similarity in the flowers as well. Note expecially the tulip-shaped flower on the 7th cent. BC jug (visible bottom left on fig11) as compared with the blue ones on the 17th cent. AD plate. (Fig.10) How can these similarities be explained? In both cases there are Eastern motifs that have been introduced to Greece at different points of her history. In the East, we can postulate a continuous tradition from the times of Abraham until modern times through various peoples, Sumerians, Assyrians, Persians, Arabs, Turks. The tradition was probably handed down from one generation to another in textiles; note that the rich decorative patterns we see on the Lindian plates are very reminiscent of embroidery and weaving.

52

The street and the entrance to old houses.

In 1929, a factory was founded in Rhodes, which started imitating the old tradition. The resulting plates are very popular and characteristic of Lindos and can be found in most tourist shops in Rhodes. They are «folkloristic», that is they imitate a genuine tradition without being themselves a genuine ofshoot of it. Nevertheless, these plates are very attractive and can be used both as decoration for the walls (they have holes on the back) or as dinner plates.

Cobbled street in Lindos. In the background the Acropolis.

The Bell-tower of the church
of Panaghia (Virgin Mary).
The Acropolis can be seen in
the background.

A view of the village of Lindos from the Acropolis.

House with Lindian Plates: There is an old house in Lindos which exhibits traditional plates, and where one can buy the modern versions also. You will find this house on your right on the way up to the Acropolis. It has a sign: «Old House with the Famous Lindian Plates». This house is a live museum as well as a tourist shop. It was built in the 15th or 16th cent. AD, and it supposedly belonged to a family of captains. The ceiling is especially beautiful, decorated with floral motifs reminiscent of the plates. Note also the bridal area on a raised dais. According to the owner, this is not where the newly wed couple slept, but where the bride's dowry was exhibited. The house includes a «house shrine» an area where the family icons, some of them very old, are kept. The old plates are hung on the wall as they were also hung in the old times, serving a decorative function.

An old house of the nobility with Lindian plates.

11. *Rhodian vase of «Phikelloura» type.*

10. *Lindian plate.*

The Church of Panaghia (Virgin Mary).

The Byzantine Church of Panaghia: In the centre of the village stands the church of Virgin Mary, the Panaghia. It was built in the 14th cent. AD, but some additions were made later. It is cruciform in shape with a large octagonal dome, a simple and yet effective plan. The altar screen (templo in Greek) is made of wood, exquisitly carved, and is said to have been made in the 17th cent. AD. The paintings are in the Byzantine tradition but are the work of an 18th cent. artist. They are arranged into panels with scenes from the life of Christ and Virgin Mary. The birth of Christ, his Presentation to the temple, his crucifixion and Resurrection are some of the scenes. Interesting are scenes of Hell (immediately

*The interior of the church of Panaghia
(Virgin Mary).*

to the left of the door as you are facing the altar) and Paradise (to the right of the entrance). Finally, the zoomorphic portrait of Saint Christopher is worth pointing out. He has a head reminiscent of a dog or jackal. According to the story, Christopher was a very handsome youth and every girl fell in love with him. He was constantly under the pressure of temptation and therefore asked God to change his form so that he would not appear so beautiful any more. God listened to his prayers and changed him into an animal. This is an interesting reversal of the fairy tale of the Beauty and the Beast transformed into a Christian tale. St. Christopher is on the lower tier on your right as you are facing the altar.

Enchanting beach at Lindos.

The Bays: Lindos has two beautiful bays: Megalos Ialos (big bay) and Mikros Ialos (small bay) which is better known as St. Paul's bay. The large bay lies to the N. of the Acropolis and has many attractions: a lovely beach with umbrellas and beach-chairs as well as some good restaurants. It is also a very good harbour and served as such in antiquity. The mythological tradition connects it with the arrival of Heracles' son Tlepolemos, who stopped here with his companions on his way to Asia Minor. The myth points to the importance of the geographical position of Lindos **en route** to Asia Minor. This bay with its sandy beach can be reached from the square of the village by a narrow road which connects the two directly.

St. Paul' bay is very small, it almost resembles a lake. It is even more

Enchanting beach at Lindos.

picturesque than the large bay and lies to the S. of the Acropolis. According to tradition, St. Paul stopped there when he was being transported to Rome by boat to be tried. A tempest almost sank the ship, but then, almost by a miracle, the small bay was discovered and catastrophe was avoided. A small chapel on the bay commemorates St. Paul's visit. You can get a very good view of it when standing on the S. edge of the Acropolis, near the temple of Athena Lindia.

The Acropolis: The Acropolis (literally translated: the city at the top) is the most conspicuous feature of the landscape. This rocky hill is naturally fortified; it is almost triangular in shape with a surface of 8400 m^2. The buildings on it span

*The stone ship, carved on the rock of
the acropolis of Lindos.*

*The entrance to the Acropol
of Lindos.*

*A section of the Doric Stoa and the Byzantine
church of St.John.*

many centuries. If we take the remnants of a 6th cent. BC staircase into account,
we have every period represented from the 6th cent. BC, onwards, down to the
period of the Knights. The most obvious remnants come from this latter period,
especially since the fortifications, built by the Knights, are so impressive. The hill
must have been fortified in antiquity as well, but not very strong walls would have
been needed then. It was the increasing threat of the Turks that forced the Kni-

ghts to strengthen their fortress.

One enters the Acropolis through the Medieval fortfication gate, where one buys the entrance ticket. After climbing a few steps, one reaches a platform with two interesting monuments on the left of the visitor, as he moves up toward the Medieval palace. One is a **semicircular dais** (exedra) with an inscription about a certain Aglochartos, who was a benefactor of the sanctuary of Athena because he

67

donated olive trees. The inscription dates from the 3rd or 4th cent. AD. Presumably this was a family monument of Aglochartos, and it was used for family cult. In the middle there is a rectangular slab which was the family altar. There is a niche in the centre of the monument for the accommodation of a statue.

To the right of the semicircular dais, there is a **carving of a ship** from the Hellenistic period. The ship is admired because it gives a vivid impression of ships of the 2nd century BC. It is a ship of war, which would be very fast, and which had a technical name: **triemolia.** It used both sails and oars for maximum speed. It is said that this type of ship developed originally in Asia Minor by the pirates. The Rhodians, however, were able to copy the technique of making such ships and used them to chase pirates away. The ship was not carved for its own sake but as a base for a statue, now lost to us, of the admiral Hagesandros. He had distinguished himself in war, and the Rhodians honoured him with a statue, a gold wreath, and by making him president of the Games. The statue was standing on the stern of the ship, right above the inscription (which is not very conspicuous any more). Thus, the ship served as a base for the statue, but was organically connected with it: The admiral Hagesandros, larger than life-size, would appear standing on a ship. The symbolism is obvious, but there are even more details to complement the iconographical message. Towards the prow of the ship there is a rectangular block which represented the throne of the admiral. If you look at this throne from the front of the ship (you have to go very close to the rock and imagine the ship is coming towards you), you will note that the front part of the throne imitates a temple with a goddess visible inside. It is probably the temple of Athena Lindia, who granted Hagesandros the desired victory. Thus, a number of small details, which can remain unobserved by the modern visitor, connect civic virtue with piety and ultimately with the temple at the top.

Immediately to the right of the ship there are remnants of the 6th cent. BC stairway from the time of Kleoboulos.

After climbing the modern stairway, one reaches the **Medieval Commandery.** First one enters a vaulted room which was the ground floor of the commandery. There are many inscribed blocks from antiquity which, although not as interesting as the ship base, give us information of historical value. On these bases were placed the statues which stood in the sanctuary. There are also some cylindrical Roman altars, which can be recognized because they are decorated with bucrania (bull's heads).

After a second vaulted room, with more inscribed statue bases, one comes to a narrow passage. To the right there is a series of vaults. They were made in the Hellenistic period and function as substructures of the artificial terrace in front of the **Stoa or portico** (see reconstruction).

To the left there are more statue bases some of which have an interesting feature: on top they have two depressions for the fastening of the statue's feet. In the case of bronze statues, the feet could be secured by lead. To the left there is also a **semi-circular exedra** built for a certain Pamphylidas when he became priest of Athena around 200 BC. This exedra also contains an altar. The descen-

A view of the Doric Stoa.

Part of the Doric stoa on the acropolis of Lindos.

dants of Pamphylidas added statues of themselves. Even further to the left, in the N. part of the Acropolis, there are remnants of a **Roman temple,** perhaps to the deified emperor Diocletian.

The visitor now turns right, to the S., and mounts the stairway of the Doric **Stoa** or portico, which has been partially restored by the Italians. The aim of the Stoa (3rd cent. BC) was to monumentalize the entrance to the sanctuary and to

The road leading to the entrance of the Acropolis.

provide more space for the display of the numerous votives. It is symmetrical Π -shaped, a typical example of Hellenistic architecture. On the same level as the Stoa is also the church of **Hagios Ioannis,** adjacent to the commandery and dating from the 13th cent. AD.

From the Stoa, the visitor is led to the monumental staircase of the **Propylaea.** It is 21 m wide and has 34 steps. The stairway and Propylaea were built in the 4th cent. BC. to provide the appropriate entrance to the sacred ground, the temenos. Their plan was imitated by the later Stoa, so we can visualize it although no-

thing of the colonnade remains. The only traces of the Propylaea is a Π shaped base which would have given the illusion of symmetry when seen from the outside. But when the visitor entered, he would see that the right wing extended to form a series of chambers, while the left side has only a colonnade against the wall to match that. The asymmetry was dictated by the need to leave free space in front of the temple, and it is not unique. The Propylaea on the Acropolis of Athens are asymmetrical also, and there again the asymmetry is disguised. The Propylaea served many functions: They screened off impure visitors from the temenos, served as an art gallery for important works of art and, finally, they were probably used as a banquet hall.

The temple: comes into view next. Since it is placed in the corner, one does not see it **en face** but from a slight angle, so that part of the long wall is visible together with the façade. The altar would have been at the centre of the temenos, if Dyggve is right and it did exist. The temple has four columns on the short sides and was built in the 4th cent. BC.

An Ionic Stoa was built in Roman times, blocking the view towards the sea. Near the W. wall of the Propylaea a **repository** of discarded offerings was found which are valuable for the history of the sanctuary and the history of Greek cults in general. When offerings were getting too many, the priests often buried the less valuable ones, because they could not be thrown away. This is why they were discovered buried in a ritual pit.

Monuments N. of the Acropolis: Kleoboulos' Grave

On the edge of the promontory of the N. side of Megalos Ialos, a funerary monument is situated, known as the grave of the tyrant Kleoboulos. In fact this is just a popular name for it; the grave dates from the late Classical or Hellenistic period, and we don't know who was buried in it.

It is a round structure of a diameter of about 9 m. It had a rectangular burial chamber in the center, 2,10 X 4,16m, the walls of which were probably covered with stucco. The grave proper was carved into the E. side of the wall, and this is where the sarcophagus (coffin) would be placed. The monument has a conical roof. Since it is difficult to get there, except by walking, one can look at the monument from the N. side of the Acropolis. It is not really visible from that distance, but one gets an idea of the location. In Christian times the church of Hagios Aimilianos was built there.

The temple of Athena on the Acropolis.

Monuments NE of the Acropolis: The Boukopion

Practically nothing remains today of the sanctuary of the Boukopion, but it is interesting to look at the site to get a feeling for the surroundings, in which the Lindians practiced their sacrifice. It has been identified by a series of inscriptions bearing the name Boukopion, which literally means the «slaughtering of bulls» The sanctuary consisted of a small temple, some 12 m long (Fig.12) with a tripartite structure, comprising an anteroom, a cella, a backroom. This small temple must have been founded around the 8th cent. and must have been in use until the Hellenistic period, since inscriptions from that time are found there. But no pottery fragments later than the 6th cent. BC have been found. This may mean that the sanctuary declined after the archaic period.

The court in front of the small temple is very small and large-scale sacrifices cannot have taken place there. But around the edifice there are a number of ceremonial aeas, which have been identified by the presence of inscriptions. In addition, the rocks are natural platforms, where the spectators could sit, if the sacrificial ceremonies were of long duration. A large number of votives in the shape of bovids confirms the idea that the Boukopion was a sanctuary, where regular sacrifices took place. We cannot know if it was an extension of the sanctuary of Athena or if some other god was worshipped there. The Boukopion can be viewed from the N. side of the Acropolis.

Monuments to the S. of the Acropolis:
The Theatre and the Tetrastoon

The Theatre (Fig.13) is situated below the Acropolis on the S. side and is cut into the rock. It is quite close to the sea. It had 19 rows of seats in the lower part and seven in the upper part. Eight aisles facilitated traffic for the 2500 estimated spectators. Nothing remains of the stage. On a raised platform, surrounding the semicircle of the stage, the ceremonial thrones were placed for the priests of Athena. A block with the inscription «Of Athena» was found nearby, probably belonging to a throne. The theatre was thus intimately connected with the cult of Athena on the Acropolis. Traditionally, however, theatres are also connected with the god Dionysus, in whose honour the performances were held. On the S. slope of the Acropolis of Athens, for example, there stood a theatre to Dionysus, dating from the 4th cent. BC. It is thought that this Lindian theatre dates also to the 4th cent. BC.

A view of the entrance to the
Acropolis of Lindos.

dos: entrance to the acropolis.

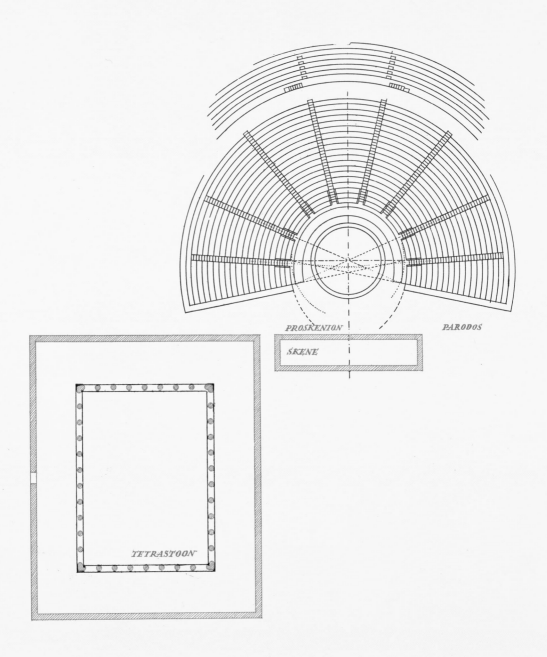

PROSKENION   PARODOS

SKENE

TETRASTOON

13. 14. *Plan of the tetrastoon (portico) and ancient theater*
of Lindos. After Dyggve.

It is well known that tragedy developed out of a song which was performed during the Dionysiac festivals. Thus cultural and religious activities were intimately associated in antiquity. In addition to dramatic performances, musical and other contests could be held in the theatre.

Next to the theatre, there was a rectangular edifice of which the base only survives today, known as the **tetrastoon** (four-sided portico). (Fig.14) This rectangular building enclosed a colonnade so that four stoas or porticoes were formed. It is generally thought that it functioned as a gymnasium, that is a place for athletic exercises. However, it is too small for such a purpose and would not fulfil the requirements for the installations normal in a Hellenistic gymnasium. Dyggve proposed another explanation: The tetrastoon was another ceremonial building intimately associated with the theatre, to which it is very close. Religious ceremonies associated with the cult of Dionysus Smintheus could have taken place there. We know from inscriptions that atheltic contests, sacrifices and musical contests were performed in connection with this god, and it is reasonable to assume that some of these activities took place in the tetrastoon, while others in the theatre. The court, surrounded by the colonnades, was quite spacious, c. 390m^2, enough for official performances. The colonnades could accommodate 1500-1700 spectators. Thus, the tetrastoon as well as the theatre were designed for cultic activities.

In Christian times, a basilica was built on top of the tetrastoon, while some of its inscribed blocks were used in the Christian building. The basilica was eventually replaced by a small church of Hagios Stephanos, the remnants of which were demolished by the Italians, so that they could excavate the tetrastoon.

Monuments W. of the Acropolis: The Necropolis

On the W. part of the Acropolis lies the necropolis of Lindos. One monument especially deserves to be mentioned: the grave known as the Archokrateion, (or Kampana) dug into the hill of Krana. The grave is dated to the Hellenistic period. It is 22m long and 4,70 m. high with 12 half-columns in the Doric order on the lower part of its façade. Above the architrave, on the upper storey, there were altars decorated with garlands and bucrania.

The façade of the grave is very reminiscent of the scenic backdrop of a theatre. Behind the entrance there was a broad room with a narrow door, which led to a square chamber with stone benches along the walls. The original burial was placed in a pit in the floor, whereas later burials were inserted in niches in the wall.

From the inscriptions on the round altars of the upper storey, we learn that the tomb was constructed for the family of Archokrates, who was a priest of Athena Lindia around 200 BC, and his wife Aristophama. A large part of the grave collapsed in 1841, but it is still possible to get a glimpse of its original monumentality.

The temple of Athena.